TELLING MY STORY:
THE JOURNEY OF A
GHETTO GIRL

Dream big! All things
are possible.

Best,
Allesley

TELLING MY STORY: THE JOURNEY OF A GHETTO GIRL

ALLESLEY OFFICER

iUniverse, Inc.
Bloomington

Telling My Story: The Journey of a Ghetto Girl

iUniverse books may be ordered through booksellers or by contacting:

iUniverse
1663 Liberty Drive
Bloomington, IN 47403
www.iuniverse.com
1-800-Authors (1-800-288-4677)

ISBN: 978-1-4620-5156-4 (sc)
ISBN: 978-1-4620-5158-8 (hc)
ISBN: 978-1-4620-5157-1 (ebk)

Printed in the United States of America

iUniverse rev. date: 10/05/2011

CONTENTS

Chapter 1

Born to be a Rebel

Chapter 2

A Slice of the Hellish Pie

Chapter 3

Loving the Unlovable

Chapter 4

Sex in the City

Oops! Sex and the Church

Chapter 5

Captive and Hell Bound

Chapter 6

Glimmer of Hope

Chapter 7

"Adam Where Art Thou?"

DEDICATION

For my mother, Imogene!

You are a wonderful woman and a dear friend.

PREFACE

You may not know me. You may not even like me, but you can believe me that there is a conflict raging between good and evil. Unfortunately, we are all a part of this great conflict. The battle is hinged on the theme of worship—worship of God or worship of Satan, His rival and archenemy.

The King James Version of the Bible cites "And the four and twenty elders and the four beasts fell down and worshipped God that sat on the throne, saying, Amen; Alleluia." Revelation 19:4. To ignore this is to result in your eternal demise and that's a probability that none should gamble with. It's just too important that we understand that our Savior and Lord, Jesus Christ is doing all He can to save us but, we must desire to be saved.

My prayer and hope for all of us living in such treacherous and evil times is that we will sense our need for God and the nearness of His glorious coming and become needy of His saving grace and greedy for a place in His eternal kingdom. Therefore I say unto you, what things soever ye desire, when ye pray, believe that ye receive them and ye shall have them. Mark 11:24 (King James Version).

Lovingly, Allesley

ACKNOWLEDGEMENTS

By the time this book comes out there would have been many persons who have contributed to its successful completion.

To My Co-Author, my Supreme Provider and Instructor Jesus Christ who became my Husband when I was rejected and abandoned. Thank you for being there and loving me in spite of me. I love You Lord and I've learnt to trust in You. This book is dedicated to You God, to bring You Honor and Glory. All this is for You Lord!

To all my family members who have challenged and annoyed me but I know there is love in all your hearts for me I love you all and share this with you. Yes Andre! If I make some money you'll get some.

To friends who have journeyed with me and have not found it easy but have stuck with it, much love to you all Ava, Petol, Paulette and Lorenza, I just had to call you by name. Special thanks to Diona!

Last but of course not least, to the praying women who helped me to discover who I am in the body of Christ, my sisters at the Restoration NOW Ministry. You all who have laughed and cried with me, this is for you!!! Remember on the 5th of July 2005, you invested in this book in cash, prayers and motivation. Thank you, Nelma, Yvonne, Jodi, Pearl, and Alecia you are my strength and my song. One love!

To my editing and publishing team from iUniverse who worked tirelessly to make my manuscript a readable material; I sincerely want to say thanks for making my dream of being an author a reality.

"OUR GREATEST GLORY
CONSISTS NOT IN NOT
FALLING, BUT IN GETTING
UP EVERYTIME WE FALL".

ANONYMOUS

1 BORN TO BE A REBEL

My whole life I have wanted to be loved. I have struggled with the insatiable need for man's love and approval and wrestled with my Savior's love. The Creator of the universe had always loved me, but I never truly believed or understood the depth of His love. That is, until my life became a suicidal travesty.

I have been a teacher for the past 15 years, both in Jamaica, where I was born and in the U.S. where I currently reside. In my classroom I shine. My light radiates and my students over the years have blessed me with their love and acceptance. I was never able to do that for myself—embrace who I am and what I have done with my life. In the past, I have selfishly believed that if I was someone else, then I would be special. I think it's a result of the memories that have never faded, drifted into the back drop of my mind and buried forever. I hope that writing this book is one way I can finally silence the voices in my head that tell me every day I am living a lie. That I am still the fragile, unkempt girl I was that I am not the overcomer I proclaim myself to be. Therefore, I am facing me! I am now willing to admit that most of my life I have desired to take my life; that I have been afraid almost every day that today would be the day I commit suicide. How scared I have been to be lonely, hurt, depressed or overwhelmed out of fear that I would succumb. This is for me and every other woman just like me who has been abused and has forgotten how beautiful she is. Here is my story!

It might have been an ordinary day in the summer of 1974, but something extraordinary was happening. On August 3rd, a baby was about to be born to a twenty-one year old unwed mother of two children, Ann and Marie. Ann was the eldest and she was my half sister, Marie and I shared the same father. My mother would have been a mother of four children at that time had she not lost her first two children to untimely deaths. Her circumstances did not call for another child, as a matter of fact, the relationship had turned abusive and she had to flee from her nemesis and baby-father before the pregnancy was full-term.

Notwithstanding, the torrid affair that they had, she wanted to be a mother once again, so in the bathroom in a tenement yard she gave birth to her third child. She was a baby girl weighing in over nine pounds. There was not much to look forward to but providing for this child amidst all the turmoil she faced. Eventually she started to make amends with her child's father. But when things remained stormy and tempestuous between them, she decided to leave for good. It may have been due to the fact that yet another man had not given her the love, respect and care that she so desperately needed. It is hard to tell what goes on in the minds of women who love their baby-daddies in spite of the abusive nature of their relationships.

Initially my toddlerhood was good, except for one snag—I went to basic school an early childhood center at the age of three years old and experienced my first case of abuse, when I was pushed by another student and subsequently broke my left arm. This however, would not be the last case of physical abuse that I would have to endure.

Prior to this, my mother had relocated to the island's capital and she now resided in an inner-city community in the volatile Kingston 13 area. She had a new beau and was very much captivated by his mystique and charm. He also had an advantage. He loved me and I guess if he was capable of loving another man's child, he was a good candidate to be a step-father.

The loving family ties and times did not last because when I was a little over 3 years old my father asked that I spend some time with him in the country, an urban parish named Clarendon. This became a decision that my mother made that we would both regret. I did not just spend the Christmas holiday with my father but what seemed to be a lifetime. I did not go back to live with my mother until I was eight years old.

Living with my father is one of the hardest things I have ever done. He was rough and showed meager portions of love or approval for my sister, Marie, and me. The experiences ranged from wicked to ridiculous and I don't know how he got away with it all.

My sister Marie was already living with our father and when I joined. She was the only reason I was happy. My father is a diminutive man who possessed great strength and had immense anger issues. I have since had dialogue with some of his siblings and discovered that he too had an unbearable childhood. I think I have finally forgiven him for the pain and anguish he has caused me and I am trying to move on. In the country, we were the last house on the street, we lived next to the train tracks and I would listen to the trains go by and dream. After you crossed the train tracks you would be greeted by the swift waters of the Rio Cobre River. I still can hear the trains roaring on the tracks and I still vividly see the raging waters that churned nearby. I go back now and then in my mind and try to find good memories that make me feel proud of my father, I go back.

The irony of it all is that I go back to childhood in spite of how difficult it was. They are my precious memories and no matter how hard I try not to remember, I often do.

My father was a great cook. He would see to it that we had our meals once he was around but when he wasn't, we were not allowed to eat the food in the house. That was so crazy to me that we could not eat the fresh bread or drink the milk. If we did and we often did, we were beaten very badly. After so many beatings, we finally began to rely a lot on neighbors to assist us with food when daddy was not around and that came with a tremendous price.

Our home in the country belonged to my uncle who worked on a cruise ship in the Bahamas and was away six to eight months at a time. My father played the caretaker role for his brother's estate. I think it was something my father resented doing. There were three rooms that were leased to male tenants who over the years became a part of our lives. There was the aspiring reggae artist and his brothers. They supplied us with hot meals regularly and provided home-made remedies when I had ear aches in the middle of the night. It is so funny how they got us to jump through hoops for food. We had to play games like eating a hot scotch bonnet pepper to show how much we needed something to eat. Scotch bonnet peppers are one of the hottest types of pepper on the island.

Then there was the tailor who had two sons. He would bring goodies for us for small favors. Every time he brought us tasty treats to eat he fondled and groped us. He was so old, almost like a grandfather to me and my sister. It was so disgusting to have his hands touch my skin. His hands were coarse and full of calluses from years of tailoring. He showed no remorse.

There was also the baker who had delicious cakes and a caring spirit. When he left, he took with him a big piece of my heart because he never interfered with us children. He always wanted to look out for our best interest, but, something went wrong as it sometimes do and he left under trying circumstances.

Among all the memories I have of my childhood the most vivid ones are of my father and how badly he treated us. He used electric wires to beat and scar us and sometimes these beatings took place while we were sleeping and especially if we wet the bed. I guess to him the ends justified the means.

My father had an excellent stone throwing mechanism. He would just let it fly and wherever it hit, however painful it was, you stayed hit.

We were more or less terrified of our father. I mean fear consumed me, to the extent that I hated him for a long, long time. The times I was even remotely happy were when he sang to us. I sometimes still imagine him sitting by the outside wood fire singing Ray Price's song "Lay Your Head On My Pillow". Those were happy times when his rich tenor voice fell in sweet melodious tones on my ears, and I wanted to lay my head on my father's shoulders knowing that I was daddy's girl.

Times in the country provided me with an eye opening view of some harsh realities of life. Death was a crippling reality for me as I experienced the tragic death of school mates taken by the unforgiving Rio Cobre River. Domestic violence riveted our home as my father fathered many children with different mothers over a period of time and most if not all the relationships ended badly.

Then there was the void of being unloved especially by the man that should love you the most as you are a part of him interwoven and taken from his being. When you look like him you have his toes and his nose yet he doesn't notice you and if he does he really doesn't care. What was missing during childhood: love from my father! I never truly felt my father's love and because of this I never truly understood my Heavenly Father's love. I believe now that this set a trend in motion that would affect my life for a long time.

Childhood had many growing pains not only at home, but at school. I was called "granny" because I carried my aunt's old bags to school and wore the worst cheese bottom shoes possible. Little could be said for my deportment and maybe even about my personal hygiene. I performed poorly in school, behaved badly and seemed to be dumber than everyone else. I was not much to look at either, in my mind. To me, I looked hideous and most times felt even worst.

Over the years I would fantasize about my mother—her beauty, her strength, her wisdom. When she came to visit, it was the best time ever. She did the best she could by coming to see us every now and then and bringing gifts. I loved her when she came and missed her when she was gone. She looked so beautiful each time I saw her that I could hardly believe she was my mother.

It seemed as if every time she came when she left my father was worst than before. I often wondered about it looking back maybe he still loved her but could not make it work and I guess now I don't even want to know.

What is the sense of it all anyway? I don't know that they would have made it and I don't know how different my life would have been so I am learning to be happy with how things are and hope that they turned out the best they could under the circumstances! There was also the fear of attachment. It was a struggle. This happened because once my sister and I loved this little rejected pet chicken and we called it Seven. We searched all over for our beloved pet and could not find it anywhere. After having our dinner, our father told us that the meat we had eaten was our beloved friend Seven. That still makes me feel sad to this day!

Forming friendship was a struggle as well. We had a close childhood friend named Maggie. I have not seen her in over twenty years. I hope wherever she is that life has been kind to her because my father wasn't. My sister and I loved her dearly like a sister, but our father drove a wedge between us and we really could not understand why. He told us Maggie was a 'fast girl' and she was not a good girl to be friends with. It took a few years for her to tell us why our father did not want us to be her friend. He was having sex with her, a minor! So not only was my father the one I feared, he was now the one I hated. My sister and I cried and cried because there was nothing else we could do. That was something that really changed me forever. That he could hurt a friend like that who was a child! That he could help to steal all her innocence like that! I often wondered if he would ever do that to my sister or to me.

I was embarrassed to admit that even though my father never molested my sister and me, there were times after learning about the incident between him and my friend that I wondered if he would. That's a terrible thing for a child to feel or even think about!

While my friend had been molested by my father, I had been molested by a step-sister when I was five years old and again by a family friend. Shortly, after entering the 4th grade, I went to live in Kingston with my mother, step-father, my eldest sister Ann, and two younger brothers, Christopher and Samuel. My sister Marie would remain in the country with my father for another couple years. Although, I lived with my mother, I had to spend summer holidays with my father. I could not understand how my mother allowed that to happen, but it did. We had to spend summers with our father so that he would help my mother out with financial support. While spending summer holidays with my father, I was molested by one of his friends on my 11th birthday. This family friend told me earlier that day that he had a special gift for a very special birthday girl. I was so excited and expectant. It turned out to be an unforgettable gift.

Later that night, I fell asleep watching television in my uncle's living room. I awoke to find this family friend kissing me, and I had never been kissed before. He kissed and caressed me for a long time. He used his hands to cover every inch of my tender 11 year old frame and he took my breath away when he rubbed between my legs. I closed my eyes out of shame, pain and fear. I wanted to die. No, I think I died! He told me that this was my birthday gift and I should keep it a secret because it was the best gift he could give. Only special girls deserved it he said.

When he was vehemently satisfied and through with me, I ran to get my older sister and told her what this man, this monster had done and we wept. Our father was out doing night fishing on the calm Rio Cobre River. We huddled together and waited for morning to come and the nightmare to be over. The next morning, I told my father and he did nothing. I was shocked!

My father was dismissive and was not concerned at all about the degrading details I shared with him. That is something I will never forget and I will take with me to the grave. In retrospect, I think that's where my love affair began with suicidal thoughts and images. I considered letting the Rio Cobre River wash away my body. I had seen bodies pulled from the river and I had mourned for those who met untimely and tragic end. Now I wanted to be a recipient of the river's wrath and fury. I thought of just lying on the train tracks and allowing the train to roar over me and put an abrupt end to my pain. I think I was too young and scared to die alone.

Sexual abuse became a part of my life and it greatly affected my self esteem and my self-worth. My emotions ranged from self loathing to increased suicidal thoughts from my early teens into adulthood. There were times when I would just imagine my death and my demise, sadly, that would be the only time I felt happy. I often thought the only reason I was born was to die. That was my life! How would I eventually end my life? I struggled with this fantasy/reality in my head and yet nobody knew. Or nobody wanted to know!

2 A SLICE OF THE HELLISH PIE

Childhood can be a period of immense joy that should be savored and then it can be a period that you spend your entire adulthood trying to forget. When I turned 10 years old I bloomed and blossomed into training bras and menstrual cycles. Adolescence came upon me like a bull in a fighting ring. It was ferocious and I was unprepared. I had faced a cruel father, and many instances of sexual abuse. Nothing had prepared me for what was to come.

Living in an inner city community has its perks I have been told, I frankly don't know of any. I have seen murders go unsolved because no one would talk! I have seen women battered by their baby fathers. I have seen my own sister engaged in physical altercations with her own baby daddy. The poverty is unrelenting; I have had to wear other people's clothes and shoes because my parents were not able to buy what I needed. I shared the same bed with my brothers and sisters through the years. Teenage pregnancy was and still is a current affair, and it's stylish and trend-setting, to be honest. Thank God that cup passed from me. There are the occasional neighborhood watches because thieves and other predators were on the prowl. Funerals and mourning are so vivid in my mind; I can almost remember all the dates and names. Those stabbed to death or shot to death, those who were gang raped and tormented and could do nothing about it.

Inner city living was tragic, but God must have been with me and my family. I was so shapely and mature in body that I was pursued by many pedophiles in my community by the age of 10. I was groped on the way to school or to the grocery shop, sometimes by older men who were fathers themselves and/or even friends of the family. I often wondered if that's all I was—an object to be fondled at will. That did something to my mind and it took God's love and therapy to deliver me.

My step-father had a nephew, who was older than my siblings and I. He taught me how to french kiss. He even counseled me when I did well and maneuvered me when I missed the mark. Back then, at the age of 12 it seemed so normal. Now, I find it quite disturbing and evil.

Somehow through all of this I went from primary school to a traditional high school. I was successful in my Common Entrance Examinations (now known as the Grade Six Achievement Test-GSAT). I would juggle life with my family in Kingston and summers with my father in Clarendon.

My mother married my stepfather in January 1988, and shortly joined a Sunday worship church congregation. We went with her to church on Sundays. Shortly after joining our new church I became active in church life and made friends with other young members of the flock. During preparation for our Easter program in 1990, something rather bizarre happened. I went to practice for the Easter program on a school night with my two younger brothers. I went to church but instead I sat outside and talked with a young man who was passing by. I felt eerie, like something was not right and I could not figure out what it was. I told the young man that I felt like I was about to die or something bad was going to happen to me and he laughed and said that it was all in my mind.

The rich reggae music filled the air, laughter and chatter were all around as people mingled with each other. Inside the church were vibrant words spoken of the Crucifixion and the unconditional love of God, but I stood outside petrified. About 9 o'clock, they called for dismissal and I was invited into the church. When I went in, the adults reprimanded me for my waywardness and insolence. By this time my temper boiled and I refused to close the session with prayer. As soon as they dismissed, I stormed out leaving everyone, even my younger brothers behind.

I walked down the street alone and veered to a lonely track to avoid any more conversations. Walking in the dark by myself, I felt I had a right to be stubborn and strong-willed. After all, no one asked me why. My thoughts were abruptly interrupted as I heard footsteps approaching, but when I turned there was no one in sight, so I proceeded alone. Within a flash this stranger was on me, with an object to my head. At first I thought it was a gun, I would later find out that it was a butcher knife. Swiftly he pulled me off the foot-path and into the nearby bushes. I tried to scream and he punched me so hard to the face the pain was instant. He kicked me and hit me like he knew me and he was mad at me. I was heaved on to a pile of filth and garbage and he began to stuff whatever he could find into my mouth for me not to scream. He yanked my clothes up and parted my legs aggressively with brute force.

He burrowed his way between my legs and all the time I wrestled and fought with all the strength I could muster. I was fitful! I mumbled and begged and he told me he was giving me what I wanted, that I asked for it. He told me that it would do me good and he was the best and he could please me. I felt the dirt, the trash beneath me; I smelled the stench of decaying animals and garbage. And here I was like a pile of garbage myself. We wrestled but, his rage was thunderous. He forced his way into me and penetrated me with force and brutality.

I remembered that my body limped after a while and I started to think how he was going to slash and kill me, right there among the dead and decaying, the debris and waste I thought he was going to slaughter me like an animal. His voice was convincing that I deserved this, that I was a sex object and I was finally getting what I deserved, after all many had touched and grope but none had raped me.

It would take the next decade or so from that day on for me to believe that I did not deserve to be raped on a pile of garbage on an infested patch of land. I remembered thinking that I was a dog. His hands were so unforgiving; his breath was all over me. He united his body with mine and tried to find a rhythm all his own. He made me feel sick and disgusted. Who was he? Was he clean or a carrier of some sexually transmitted infection? So many things race through your mind when you are in danger! Why is this happening to me? Was one of the questions that would not leave my mind. I tried bargaining and reasoning with him, but it was not to be. In the heat of the moment, bystanders or on-lookers that had seen or heard the scream cried out for help and before the next phase of the attack took place gun men came and chased him away. Yes I was being raped and I was rescued by unlawful men with guns. Members of my church, including my two younger brothers, came and took me home where we had to tell the news to my parents. The next day my mother took me to the doctor while the family gathered and cried. We read Psalms and prayed.

After that it was not mentioned or discussed again. I went to school and acted normal, but that was too hard even for me. It definitely took its toll on my mental and physical health. Soon I was having fainting spells and my suicidal thoughts became more and more prominent. After a year of being so sick and unstable my mother took me to the doctor and I was referred to the Psychiatric Unit of the University Hospital of the West Indies for evaluation and scheduled for counseling. I went with my mother for my first counseling session and I felt quite weird. The session began with my mother telling the doctor of her pregnancy with me and included information about pre-natal and post-natal care, how I lived with my father in the country and different things they thought had triggered my downward spiral. My mother mentioned the incident that took place one year prior and I lost it. For the first time I screamed and cried like something life changing had really happened. I sobbed for a long time and let the flood gates of grief and sorrow open. I would go for counseling for another couple years until my doctor thought he should tell me I was okay to go and face the unknown. He actually told me that he believed I would be okay. I guess he saw something that only God saw in me. A person! A complicated individual! Through all that I have been through, I am loved by an ever loving God. He has walked with me when I stumbled from day to day and He believes there is an amazing person on the inside. I am not a dog, though I thought I was and I never deserved to be raped or abused in any way. It is not my fault and I am not responsible for the evil that men have done or will do. I was a victim and now I am a victor, an overcomer of some of life's unforgiving moments.

Many persons experience rape and sexual abuse every day. It sometimes happens on the job, at school or even in the home. God never intended for His beloved people to experience these tragedies of sin, but it happens. However, His love is un-ending and unfailing and He will always take care of His beloved children.

All these experiences, though traumatic and daunting, have helped to shape my destiny in one way or another. They have caused me pain and much grief and allowed me to go on a self destructive path of low self-esteem and loss of identify. They have even helped to cripple my growth as a sexual being.

For a long time I thought I was a sex object used for pleasure or for some sexual gratification. Now I have embraced the fact that I am a spiritual being and a sexual being, as well and that in both entities of myself I am beautiful.

I have since proclaimed God to be a Restorer and a Repairer of the breach. I have prayed a simple prayer: Lord I have lost my youth, my virginity, but, I ask You for restoration of my body and my mind. Restoration of my morals and give me Your esteem so I will no longer feel like a dog or less than I am or should be. I believe it and receive it in Your precious name, Amen.

If you, like me, have experienced any type of abuse whether physical, sexual or verbal, God can restore and give you His esteem. You are beautiful! Do not worry that you are too old or that it is too late for you. It is never too late for the Lord to do His restorative work in your life as He stated in Isaiah 41:13, "For I the Lord thy God will hold thy right hand, saying unto thee, Fear not; I will help thee."

3 LOVING THE UNLOVABLE

In the summer of 1991 I was busy picking up the pieces of my life. I no longer thought about the words rape, beaten, and hurt. I was learning new words like horse racing, bet and Caymanas Park. I had stopped going to church and was now enjoying my carefree summer job at one of the Betting shops on Spanish Town Road. The shop was crowded with men young and old, drunkards, those who would swear on their mothers' heads, and those who were just trying to change their luck. The young man behind the counter with me was generous, kind, and almost gentle. I grew fond of him like an older brother. He taught me how to write the bets and how to listen for a winner. There was always someone with the inside scope on which horse was going to win. It was fun, but it was brief. I had been around men who for the first time were more interested in the race horses than they were in me and I liked it.

Coming home from my job I noticed a tent erected in my community. It was yet another church about to launch their evangelistic campaign; they were there to seek the lost, the forgotten and the needy. I was too ashamed to go back to my church after the rape, because everybody knew. So I stayed away!

When the crusade began I realized these people were different, but strange. They called themselves Seventh-day Adventist and they proclaimed that they had the latter day truth. I visited maybe a week into the crusade and I laughed. I laughed at how they sang and rejoiced as if everything and everyone was okay. I laughed at their "Amens", and "Hallelujahs". Soon my laughter and lack of respect was noticed by a bible worker named Sis. Eden. She introduced herself to me and soon to my family.

She was almost like a hound. She became a frequent visitor to our home. She talked with me and I grew very fond of her. After a few weeks, she led me into baptism. My younger brothers at this time had already gotten baptized and somehow that encounter led my family into the Seventh-day Adventist church.

At the crusade I met and befriended a young man who I had known for a long time but had never had conversations with. Shane and I went to the same elementary school but, he was two years older. I had now joined his church and so we became friends.

They say opposites attract, however, people with similarities can share a unique bond. Earlier that summer I had graduated from high school and was looking to venture into the world and make my mark. I remember wanting to become a nurse and hoping that I had done well enough in my exams to secure a place in one of the island's prestigious nursing schools.

I got baptized and I stopped working at the Betting Shop. My new friend, Shane, and I talked about everything. For the first time I could just be myself and tell another person some of the most private things I had been through. He was an avid listener and would occasionally chime in about how happy he was that I was okay. Before I knew it, I had fallen hard. I was in love.

He accepted me with all my flaws and even though I was still an out-patient in the hospital's psychiatric unit he never said a mean word about it. He was never judgmental, and was always supportive and reliant.

He must have been too nice to me because I asked him to be my boyfriend and he said no. I had offered myself and I was refused and I felt rejected. I lashed out at him and told him he would miss the time of his life. He was noble and he walked away from me with his head held high. That night tears were on my pillow and I don't recall having cried as hard as I did that night. I was consoled by my step-brother Samuel. He was my best friend and he too had his own story of heartbreak to share.

Although I thought it was the end it turned out to be the beginning! When he came to see me the next day he told me his girlfriend at the time was now pregnant with another man's child. I was elated and that's how our relationship began.

We saw each other every day. It was easy and convenient and we seemed to be enjoying our selves. One thing that endeared me to him was that he was suicidal and had faced a lot of personal crises and obstacles in his life. He could sometimes be cold but I saw that he could be more than that. Prior to starting our relationship he had planned to commit suicide using a cylinder of gas. He planned to turn the gas on and lock himself in the room while the air became contaminated with carbon monoxide. I was able to talk him out of going through with it. I had found in him someone I could rescue and desperately hoped we would end up rescuing each other. He swiftly became the love of my life, the center of my joy and that was not all. I would start to dream about him rather than suicide. I was mesmerized by him! Instead of forming horrid fantasies of death in my head, he became my fantasy. I was more than infatuated!

Our relationship was deep and though we had a mutual friend who encouraged the relationship, we grew to love each other on our own. I could share my deepest thoughts with him and he shared much of his hurt with me. The passion between us continued to grow. He knew my soul and eventually, he knew the contour of my body. We were so passionate about each other that a fire grew and I lusted after him and when I was not with him I was near crazy. I was desperately growing to love him without reserves.

He became my best friend, my confidant and later my lover. We could talk but more than talking we could make out in my mother's yard. We hardly did dating stuff like go on movie dates and any such thing but, once I was with him everything would be okay. I think instead of finding myself with him I continued to spiral into somebody I never grew to love or even to like very much. How could that be, how was I willing to love everybody else except God and myself?

The ecstasy could not be denied and sometimes we played games just so that we would try not to touch each other. Amidst his implosive and explosive anger and my depression, things seemed to be ideal for us; well especially, for me.

When I was nineteen years old and we were finally alone, we made love for the first time. After almost two years of thirst, we found satisfaction at long last. That sealed it for me that he was the one that I wanted to spend the rest of my life with. He knew me and I loved being with him and I thought it would last forever. Even after he went off to college and I was left behind I still loved and missed him desperately. We would write letters and try to compose poems sharing how we felt about each other.

The relationship continued to blossom even though it was experiencing some strain from his family, especially his mother who disapproved of our relationship. She did not want him fathering any illegitimate children especially with what she considered to be a poor broken girl like me. Ignoring of her insistence that we stop the relationship, we continued to deny her of the privilege of winning. We continued to have a sexual and intense affair and we decided we would eventually get married in spite of parental displeasure.

Sadly, this would not be the case. By the time I went off to college, the cracks were beginning to show. The constant bickering and harassment were taking a toll on both of us so I made a decision to break off the relationship and move on with my life. We were both angry at the people who fought against us, each other and at ourselves. That began the period of hard angry sex that took years to stop.

I may have broken off the relationship with my mouth but I couldn't with my heart and we paid the price for that with our bodies. We went our separate ways each going to college to finish what we had started and we tried to be okay. We even began to see other people, which was particularly hurtful for me because I had suspected that he had been seeing that particular girl long before. Although we had both mastered the art of betrayal, I felt betrayed.

Although, we were seeing other people when we came home for holidays we still saw each other. We would still make out and make love and I would cry and cry after the fact. What made it so heart wrenching is that we would make love one night and the next day I would see him and his new girlfriend, whom his mother very much approved. Now, I often ask myself how did I live like that or rather why?

The devil told me a lie and I believed him. I told my ex-boyfriend that "whatever the future held he would always be the love of my life." He told me the same. We lived that lie seeing others and seeing each other on and off for almost ten years. We hated each other but when we were in each others arms the hate dissipated. We argued constantly about who hurt who but when we kissed the arguments ceased and this was the way it was. We had sabbaticals. We even went years without talking and then if he looked at me long enough we were back together.

I had my first birthday party when I turned twenty-five years old. Shane invited himself to the party although we had long silenced our emotions for each other, by the night's end we were together even though my boyfriend at the time was at the party. I quickly sent him away so that I could be with my first love. Our time of silence was no more. We rediscovered each other that night only to find out as we often did that it would not last.

By this time though, the disapproval came from our voices as we both felt we were trying to recapture something that over the years we had already lost—love and respect for each other. So in vain we tried, and reluctantly we conceded. This came about because I found out that this man who I had loved and hated for so long was not who I or even who he thought he was. Over the years, of on again-off again re-runs, I became a joke. Something he did for fun and amusement. He would tell mutual friends very personal things about me and aired all my secrets that I had entrusted to his keeping. He had been doing it for years and finally he was exposed! I was mortified to think that every intimate detail of our relationship was now public knowledge and I had become the butt of every joke. He had done so many little things that I excused or forgave him for but this was unforgivable. How could I ever trust him again I wondered and I cried for what seemed like weeks. He had allowed his girlfriend to ride in the same car I was in; he ignored me in public while he slept with me in private. The man I thought would change my life almost ruined my life.

I felt crazy, lost, embarrassed and even ostracized. My mother saw my pain and my shame and she prayed with me and for me. God helped me not to take my life. I think the only reason I lived was because I was too angry to die.

Prior to all of this, I visited his college campus with a girl friend of mine. We looked at each other and he walked pass me like I wasn't even there. I had trusted him to give me self-esteem and self-worth and instead I had given over myself to the enemy. I thought he was my savior and it turned out he almost destroyed me. I had forgotten that God was the creator of all flesh! I put my entire worth in the hands of a man and found that for him I was of little or no worth. Over the years, the pain from the relationship had accumulated. I felt cheap, empty and abandoned. I wanted a man! I felt that I needed to be loved by a man no matter what or no matter whom. I knew I experienced insanity!

I became sickly, depressed and most of the time I did not have the desire for life. My will was broken and there was no resolve. I found myself in and out of the hospital. I even had to undergo both physical and psychological examinations.

I began labeling myself as a manic depressed individual. I had severe anemia and bouts of fainting spells that earned me many trips to the hospital's Emergency Room. On a couple occasions, I was admitted for brief stays in the hospital. I was labeled unstable and vulnerable because of all the things that I had gone through from childhood until now. Sometimes I feel like I must have been crazy to continue the way I did for so many years; especially, in a relationship that was as rocky and stormy as a ship on a tempestuous sea.

Though I was discussed, laughed at, mocked, jeered and ostracized, I went back each time may be for the sex or for the friendship that we had in the beginning. Maybe I longed to recapture that and refused to see that it was lost in all the rendezvous we had, we lost sight of what was important. Sometimes love really isn't enough there just needs to be more. Both of us were unlovable and we kept on trying to love. We were caught up in the desires of the flesh. Our own lust and would not let each other go free. A soul needs to be free in order to truly love. It cannot be forced or coerced or else it becomes an undesirable thing that consumes you and eventually destroys you.

How did I survive it, but for the grace of God!?!

After all this and then some, I eventually married him!

4 SEX IN THE CITY OOPS! SEX AND THE CHURCH

The night I gave my life to Christ, I was the only candidate for baptism. I thought that my life would change not just for the good, but for the better.

Outside of being molested and raped I had never entered into a consensual sexual relationship. I would enter and re-enter many sexual encounters all the while professing to be a child of God.

In this life with all its uncertainties and ongoing catastrophes and the battles that are constantly raging in our lives, there are many things that we think we want or think we need. We often learn that there are things in our lives that we can simply do without. Through all vicissitudes of my life my longing or hunger for love, affirmation and attention came or manifested themselves in horrible and detrimental ways.

After my on again and off again relationship with my first love, Shane finally ended I became hooked on sex. I have had five sexual relationships all while being a professed child of God. Fornication and lust knew my name and my address, this was one sin I had no cure for.

It began while I was enrolled in the Fall of 1993 at one of the best Teachers' College in the western hemisphere. After breaking loose and now boarding away from home and even from my religious orientation, I started to reassess my desires for love and companionship. It was not quickly but, after having one and two dates with different guys I eventually became interested in a young man who appealed to me. We were college mates but I was his senior. We would chit chat a lot initially and seemed to really like each other. We even went to school functions together. My friends and I made a bet to really enjoy our final year at school. I desired to have fun; by going clubbing, having sex on the college grounds on his dorm when it was forbidden for females to be seen on the male dorms. I wore jewelry, and scantily clad clothes. I went against my religious beliefs. In essence, I was enjoying myself and defying God.

Our first time together was as random as our other times together. It lacked meaning and romance. It happened so casually. One night while on campus, my boyfriend and I toured the grounds talking and cuddling and right as we got to the gymnasium he made his advancement. I was too promiscuous to deny him. We made love on the top of a table in a room that on any given day is trafficked by scores of people. On that night it became my pit stop. Oh how I was devastated and disgusted with myself! I cried so hard that the young man became terrified. That however, would not be the last of our nestlings on campus. Even after I had graduated and he remained, I would revisit the place were I got a fix and numbed all the sensation that my life was not what I or the Lord wanted it to be. Eventually, after a little over a year together and too many times sleeping with him, the hangovers of regret caused us to end our relationship that was not going anywhere.

I can also recall while attending college, dating other guys, but not steadily I even had three dates at a school event and made out with two of them in one night, the other found out and basically wrote me off as a 'bad girl', who could fault him any way because I had forgotten my morals or found out I hadn't acquired any during the time I was exposed to church life and religious teachings.

To a great extent I may have been angry with God and everyone else including myself and I was often depressed and weak, weak in the sense that I often lacked a will to live which was masked well because I may have been seen as okay I refuse to be normal because maybe those who knew me would not agree that I represented what normal was I was too sad and moody.

With all the other stuff going on in my life I ended college in the Spring of 1996 and became a teacher and I went back to church regularly; occasionally I participated in the activities of the church but I remained promiscuous as ever and diverted a lot from doctrinal beliefs. I formed another relationship on the highway to nowhere and again it became sexual in nature. The first time we were intimate was immediately after I had cooked his favorite dish and just like that with fish on the stove he took me right in the kitchen and I allowed it to happen and like clock work I sobbed uncontrollably for minutes at a time. He could not console me and he became petrified he must have thought he had met a freak. But, if he thought it he didn't say so but acted with great class and dignity and tried to reassure me I would be okay.

The relationship blossomed and we went out a lot. We spent a lot of romantic times together even going on trips in the country. Eventually, I started to feel safe in his arms. Even though I still cried when we made love, he never knew and maybe still doesn't know that every time I did go to him I left a part of me behind. I became fragmented and almost a little crazy.

My best memory of him was when I was on the northern coast of the island at a conference held for teachers. On the last day with preparations made to return home I was sitting in the lunch area having my meal when I was surprised by him. Job related travels took him to that area and he had come to take me home. That was one of the nicest things he had ever done for me. Then just as I was feeling that I could love him things fizzled out and he called to say he was ending the relationship. After many calls and urgent inquires, he told me to go back to God.

That was the best thing he ever did, but, I was angry and hurt and even more torn and ripped at all the seams and still I did not learn. I started a new type of adventure after having more and worse dates and not finding the man of my dreams, I engaged in out door hobbies such as hiking up the

Blue Mountain Trail. This became my new drug. I met new faces and found a passion for the great mysteries of God's creative prowess.

This, though, would be short lived. About my second or third trip or weekend spent in nature brought me face to face with two of the most attractive eyes I had ever seen. Without thinking, I plunged once again in sexual perversion, how I could be so loose or so lost defies me. Did I even understand the consequences of my actions or how I was affecting the path that God had for my young life.

Within weeks of meeting those beautiful hazel green eyes I was smitten. After long conversations on the phone, I convinced myself that this was a new start. Coincidentally, we met a week later at a camping site.

It did not take long for that weekend to change my life and possibly my destiny. That very weekend in the great outdoors I sealed my faith and put my lust to the test. I had simply given over myself to my own lust of the flesh. I did not know how to judge the situation morally or wisely. I lost my moral compass and it took years for God to rewire my heart and my brain. I thought I needed a man in my life and forgot that all I needed was God in my life and that He would provide the right man for me.

I once again succumbed to old habits and engaged in fornication with this young man. Each time I did, I felt empty, demoralized and defeated! It's almost as if I scattered pieces of myself away.

The relationship began with sex and ended with sex. Nothing less! Nothing more! The passion fizzled. The fire burnt out and we were left with nothing. How could there be a foundation for a relationship when there was no friendship?

How many have built relationships and marriages on a lie? The enemy has tricked us into believing that love is sex and all it ends up to be is an obsession. It often leaves us feeling unfulfilled, lewd and unloved. I have come to believe that love and marriage are tremendous gifts from God and that man has trampled and debased these gifts.

As one who was naïve enough to think that love could be chased or captured, I can truly affirm that true love is a gift from God and without God in the heart man does not know how to love. God is the source of true, unconditional love.

An old adage states "not all that glitters is gold." Who is not acquainted with this truth? Many are the mysteries of life. What drives a woman's desire for a man or a man's sensibilities for a woman? What allows us to feel out of control even to the point of recklessness? We sometimes consider the connection between a man and a woman to be one of life's greatest gifts. Everyone desires to be loved and to give love in return. It fuels us and sometimes it can even destroy us. Many have left all to pursue happiness in the arms of the 'right' man or woman. So have I! I have been embarrassed in my pursuit and I have been enticed by my pursuit. I have enjoyed my lust and scorned at it all in the same breath. I got pregnant in the midst of all my frivolity, but a child was never to be. I accidentally fell and loss my baby and was subsequently saved from confronting my demons publicly, especially to the church.

I entangled myself with a man who had a solid, stable relationship and was confronted by his girlfriend and I could not speak. I was a coward. I stood and looked her dead in the eyes and never said a word. I later looked myself in the mirror and did not know who I was or who I would become and I cried. I cried because there was no example of who I wanted to be and who I was, was not good enough.

I have often asked myself was it worth it. Dating and sleeping with different men what have I lost and what I have gained? I could answer by saying either way nothing it was just a fool's game there are no winners and losers here, but, I would be lying. I have lost more than I gained.

Proverbs 31: 10 and 11 says "Who can find a virtuous woman? For her price are far above rubies. The heart of her husband doth safely trust in her, so that he shall have no need of spoil." Proverbs 31 gives a descriptive narrative of the woman I now desire to be. I have since left my 'dirt' behind and have forged ahead with God's help and love. For a long time I lived a life that I was unhappy living. I always knew I loved God and had a desire to live a godly life, but I lacked the will and the discipline. I lied to myself and others, but more than that I tried to lie to God.

When we give away bits of ourselves, we don't get it back and we are left void and scared. But there is hope in Jesus! We can give Him all those desires that we have because He is the great desire of ages.

Sex is life. It breathes life and it is an essential and beautiful gift given to human beings by a great God, but it is not to be lit like a fire from here to there. Sex should be experienced in its holy estate in the union of marriage between a man and a woman. Unfortunately, so many of God's people are engaged in sex in the form of fornication and adultery. Now is the time to make it right. I have failed in my earlier life to live a celibate life, but now God has given me another opportunity to do this and I pray this time will be the best of times. I am a sexual being; I am also a spiritual being. Praise God!

5   CAPTIVE AND HELL BOUND

Today I marry my

Friend

The one who shares

My dreams

Life and love

The invitations were out. The gifts were wrapped, the church was decorated, and the buzz and excitement was heavy in the air. The date for the wedding had finally arrived all that I had wanted was about to come true. Who said dreams were only for fools? I believed in destiny and marrying this man was my destiny, so I thought.

The family, friends and even uninvited guests had gathered to witness the nuptials. We were getting married at long last! We put it together—the love, the friendship and all the planning and arrangements.

After being friends in our early days, messing up, and hurting each other so many times the love of my life, Shane, was back in my life, and we were getting married. To the best of my knowledge people were happy. Well, not everybody was, but I didn't care because I was finally going to get what I wanted—the fairy tale ending.

He had come back in my life like a whirlwind at the turn of the century, in the year 2000. So much had changed about him. He finally seemed as if I was his one and only and he had always been mine. He pursued me and finally captured my heart and my mind like he never left. I had my own apartment and his visits were welcomed and needed. He captivated me with every touch and I was smitten, so when he asked me to marry him I said yes.

He planned it all—a romantic dinner at a fabulous Chinese restaurant and he even asked the waiter to deliver the ring with my dessert. It was like something he adapted from a romantic movie.

So here we were on December 16, 2001 and the ceremony and celebration was on its way. There were even rain showers, which I thought solidified that our marriage would be blessed. I was a beautiful and radiant bride and for once I was also truly happy; forever and always was in sight. The road of life had many detours but I felt I was finally on track and nothing could go wrong. Little did I know how quickly things can change.

Waking up Monday morning beside my husband felt like something I could do for the rest of my life. We were so happy that we spent time in worship telling God thanks for how He had allowed us to find each other again. The week of our honeymoon, however, was telling. After the first of what would become many regular fights, my gut sank. I knew then and there that I had made a mistake. I made a self-fulfilling prophecy. I said it, "Honey, if we continue like this you and I are going to get a divorce". When I should have been over the moon, my floodgate of sorrow had begun.

It didn't take us long to realize we didn't know each other and that we loved hard, and fought harder. Our fights would leave us dazed and sometimes we would not speak to each other for days at a time. However, we tried to make a life for ourselves and hoped that in time the marriage would become solid and stable. At that time, that remained to be seen.

During the first month of marriage we both had concerns about its survival. He wanted to be loved and understood and I was afraid. I questioned if he had changed. He had lady friends that were calling all the time and I felt jealous, vulnerable and insecure. I had a gut feeling. Some might call it a woman's intuition. Whatever it was, I knew something was wrong. I urged my young husband to let us have personal time with each other for family worship and other family stuff. I think I had my foolish perspective of what my perfect family should look like or how a family should be.

After all, that was what I wanted—the perfect family that everybody else had. I saw it in the community we lived and at the church we attended I believed we could be models of what God could do in marriage and in essence, in the home.

But by the time the marriage had reached the six months mark, the situation, though it appeared to be normal was anything but. There were internal struggles and each person was wrestling with their own demons. He was trying and I felt I was trying and things would be picturesque and then things would just be hard. Really hard! The emotions were strained early on and they were never repaired. The on-going struggle was about many things: our independence of each other, our craftiness towards each other, the fact that we married and moved into my place, and always about the young lady at the other end of the telephone. I questioned her motives for calling my husband so frequently but all the time I was reassured by both parties there was nothing to be so worried about. After all, the young lady on the telephone was my brother Christopher's wife.

I knew they were too close but honestly I never suspected that they would have an affair. My sister-in-law and I were never close, but she was the mother of my nephew whom I loved dearly and she was my brother's wife. That was enough to keep up appearances and sit in worship at the same church and sometimes hang out with the same crowd of people. I went about putting ground rules in session to have her and my husband communicate less via the telephone. That just allowed them to meet in secret.

We discussed as a couple, having certain barriers to protect the marriage. He would go back to her and languished at how I tried to stifle their friendship. Eventually, I became the enemy in my own marriage. Over time, things kept building and growing and finally it was out of control.

I do not know if it is the fact that she called him at 3 am in the morning and he thought that was okay, or was it the gifts he bought her without my knowledge. No. It must have been their secret rendezvous that never stayed secret or was it all the lies? Whatever it was, I felt my husband slipping away. He slipped away and there was nothing I could have done.

I saw them together with my own eyes on a couple of occasions when they should not have been. The first time she ran when she saw me and caught a mini bus. The second time I ran because I did not know what to do. I felt defeated.

Up to this point, I do not know what hurt more. Was it their friendship or the fact that I saw when he began to love her and not me? I was his wife, but I was also a spectator when they began their odyssey with each other. Constantly my husband would reassure me everything was in my head, and then it was in the people's head. Soon it would be in my family's head.

Whatever was happening between my husband and my brother's wife took a toll on me. I threatened to leave. He begged for time and we went into counseling. That worked for a time. Our love making became passionate again and I felt at ease in his arms once more. We actually looked happy for a minute, but that was only temporary.

In fact, my nephew saw her standing naked in front of my husband in her bedroom, which he tried to deny. He kept in constant contact with her via cell phone and the home phone the telephone bills told the cryptic tales. Whatever it was I began to feel rage. One night I went at him and broke all our dishes. At this point I was clueless and I asked him to leave and he did.

I have often pondered about why we went for couple's counseling. Why did we try to no avail to make our marriage work when it could not stand? It had no foundation. We made plans with no sense of direction. We made love amidst the contention and confusion and got sick because of the stifling feuds. We cried, prayed, and told each the most heinous words we could possible use, yet we still tried to keep our heads above water.

The first time he left, I asked him to leave and when he came back I asked him to return, but why? I really felt as if I could not live without him even though living with him had been the hardest thing I had ever done. It was harder than being molested or being raped.

When my husband came home he seemed happy, changed and almost vibrant like the young man I had loved some 15 years before. It made me happy to see him breathing and it gave me a renewed purpose that no matter what I was going to stay the course. After all, was my husband really having an affair? All along he convinced me that all the circumstances were just that-circumstantial, and if I wanted the marriage to work I must believe my husband would never sleep with my nephew's mother. No he could not have done that and we were going to prove to everybody that they were wrong and all along he was right.

You can only live a lie for a very short while, because a lie is a lie no matter who tells it. Years ago before I married him he had hurt me so badly I wished I had died. Years later he would hurt me once again and this time I knew for sure I was going to die. Shortly, after moving back home my husband stopped touching me. As a matter of fact, he even stopped seeing me. He became so angry when people started rehashing and revealing things I never knew about him and my sister-in-law that I finally had to admit they were having a sordid affair. The night I accepted it, I locked myself in the bathroom and cried all night. He sat on the outside of the door and I believe he was crying too, but we were now crying for different reasons. He wanted to get out and I wanted to hold on.

After that we never touched each other again. We stopped sleeping together in the same bed. It was an unspoken revelation. I would cry and he pulled further and further away. I heard more and more stories about him and her during this time and honestly, I still do not believe all the stories were the truth. But I had to admit some of them were. I started to feel as if I was on a Ferris wheel in constant motion and I did my best to go to work and make my weekly attendance to church.

About two months after his return home, I felt trapped like an animal just waiting to be slaughtered. I could not even pray about it. Eventually, he asked me to meet with our pastor and I did. To my chagrin, he wanted the pastor to know that he and the young lady in question were in good standing with the church and would remain so, but the relationship with me was over. I was mortified! I became both suicidal and homicidal. I began plotting in my head how I would kill her and then kill myself. God was on my side because none of my plans prevailed.

Within two years of pledging our love in holy matrimony the marriage was over. We were strangers and all the love seeped away and just like he had magically come back in my life he left.

The night before he left, I cried as I watched him put his things together. As he packed them in the trunk of our car, sadness overwhelmed me. I still remember that unexplained heaviness. I stayed up that night wondering what life would be without him and as morning rolled around, he kissed my forehead, said good bye and slipped away. Just as my husband left me, my sister-in-law left my brother.

What would cause two people of devout faith to leave their spouses? Whatever, the case, our marriage was over and a new phase of my life had begun. It took two years for the enemy to send my life spiraling out of control and would take God and all the hosts of Heaven to save me.

Shortly after my husband left I made my first suicide attempt. I had become so depressed, withdrawn and lethargic that I could hardly cope with everyday activities. There would be unfinished chores, incomplete assignments and total emotional breakdowns. One day after coming home from church, I swallowed all my anti-depressants and went to sleep, hoping for the Grim Reaper. I would eventually wake up some 21 hours later angry and confused that I had not passed away.

I considered cutting my wrists, jumping from a moving car and I actually walked into oncoming traffic. The motorists swirled and cussed at me but I was left to live. I engaged in starvation and chanting and praying for death. Unfortunately nothing happened. Within the first three months after at least three trips to the Emergency Room and crying all the tears

I had to cry, I became more determined than ever that I had to die. Living seemed not to be an option, I could not even envision going on with my life. There were interventions made by family members and friends, but I had already died on the inside and I could not live the way I was.

I could not stop crying! What hurt most was not that he left me, but that he never loved me. I think that was the truth I did not want to live with. How could he marry me without loving me? I loved him. I truly believed I did. Sometimes I wonder if I still do.

When prayer and counseling did not help and I felt God was out of reach, I made my final suicide attempt. It was on a beautiful Sunday, just like when I had gotten married. I placed a combination of pills in my mouth. That decision was based on years of screw-ups!

I am still here so something dramatic must have happened, and it did. I heard for the first time the most melodious yet penetrating voice I have ever heard and the words weighed heavy on my ears and pierced my heart. "No! No! I have need for thee!"

I never got the chance to take my life and I am happy. I wish I could say I stopped crying or feeling hurt, or that my life turned out perfect after that, but it didn't. Immediately following that experience I lost my hair. I went bald, but, thank God I did not lose my life.

My husband left me for my brother's wife and I thought that it was the end of my life. Beloved, I was wrong. It was only the beginning.

6 GLIMMER OF HOPE

Call to Ministry . . .

You are called! You are called! You are called! Stop worrying. God cares so much for a bird, then what about you. Just relax in the arms of the One who can't fail. This is the text I received on my mobile phone on the 23rd of June 2005. How could she have sent such a text to me on a day when I was questioning everything about my call to work in God's ministry?

Shortly, after the separation from my husband, I became involved in prayer for my own benefit, seeking restoration from the Lord for my family. I now believed I had allowed the enemy, Satan, to come in our lives and it was now my duty to pray him out and capture my family from his hellish grasp. Little did I know that God always has a plan. I had been running from God for years for all the what ifs that had occurred in my life especially the rape I had suffered a long while back and all the scars from childhood. But, God and I were finally going to have a face to face with one of us being changed and because God is unchangeable the one in need of change was me.

Therefore, instead of seeking only prayer for me, God miraculously turned it around and gave me prayers for others. He taught me how to pray and gave me the wonderful gift of prayer and intercession that I will forever treasure because it changed my life.

My first encounter was when I met with a prayer group. I was seeking prayer for my failed marriage and my life's crisis. In turn, I was used by the Lord to pray especially for a young a man I had never met. He later confessed that all I had said was the truth. I wish I could say, though, that my troubles were no more, but this was not the case. However, the gift and the word of God grew and multiplied in my life. (Acts 12:24)

It was so hard for me to understand how I had gone into this prayer group seeking for myself and the Lord ended up using me, a depressed, suicidal train-wreck. The spirit of prayerful intercession consumed me even when I did not want or desire it. It took hold of my heart and never relinquished its grasp. Hallelujah! I would not have wanted it to anyway.

The prayers became so powerful, I felt weird. I would open my mouth and recognize my voice, but knew it had to be the heart and the words of God. I never cared so deeply to pray so fervently for people. Some I knew others I had never met. I would pray at church, on the bus to work, at work or any open space where there was need for prayer. To tell the truth I was just wondering in the midst of all this, when, would I be restored? I had met God, but I was still not like Him.

Through this medium, I started to experience the hand of God in my life, calling me. Not just calling me, but calling me to be changed from what I was into what He desired me to be. I wrestled both day and night. All I wanted was for my marriage to be reconciled and my life to be restored. I did not want to go deeper and to become consumed by God and to work for God. I wanted only what I could see and appreciate and nothing more. After all, praying for others is serious business. You may even start to love people and become concerned for somebody other than yourself and I was not willing to do all that. I believed I did not have what it took to do that.

So I rebelled and argued and doubted and pouted especially when I got the inclination that I was to resign my job and go into full time ministry. I went berserk:—literally. I ranted and raged and made attempts on my life. I figured if God was not going to give me what I wanted, I was not going to give Him what He wanted—a surrendered heart—and I felt I had that choice.

With all my persistence to defy God, after almost a decade in the classroom as a teacher, I resigned my position not with fan fares and applauds but with doubts, anguish and fear of the unknown. All this happened eight months after my husband had left. I was out of a job had no source of income and no one to take care of me. In Jamaica they say "you are on your own."

I entered a new chapter of my life that took me through mountain tops and deep dark, deserted valleys. I felt heartache and heart break all over again. After my resignation, I started the 2004 school year, in my rented side of my landlord's house on my face daily, just weeping and agonizing with God. I tried to reason, bargain and persuade God that I needed a job or at least a husband with a job to be surrendered to the thought of full time work in His ministry. None of what I asked for was granted to me. The next step was in November of 2004 I began my daily trek to the ministry's office, Restoration NOW, a Christian counseling and prayer non-profit organization. There were three of us in the office daily and we prayed and fasted almost every day.

Looking back, I think those were some of my best days on planet Earth. Prostrating before God for the souls of others. Whoever they were, we would pray for them. Whatever their concerns or problems, we interceded with God on their behalf and that would be my new 'job' for another two years.

The bills during this time would become overdue and with no monthly income I believed that I lived off God's sense of humor. The shoes fell off my feet, literally. And I went down to the last pair. The telephone was disconnected and I had an empty cupboard everyday for almost two or three years. The clothes faded and became jaded and I lost my faith over and over again. However, through this time of great uncertainty, God did marvelous work. He would send someone with groceries, or send someone else with money so one or two bills could be paid. And with all this going on I was a part-time student pursuing my Master's degree in

Educational Psychology at the University of the West Indies, Mona campus.

I remember owing one year's rent and the Lord sending me to do a devotion program at an elementary school (or Primary school as it is called in Jamaica). At the end of devotion, a staff member at the school blessed me with 80, 000 (Jamaican dollars) and I was able to pay the rent. That's how it was. I never knew what the Lord was going to do or who He was going to use to do it, but when it was done, He received all the praise, honor and glory.

When my underclothes were torn and ragged he allowed my landlady to get some from the United States and they were not her size so she gave them to me. She never knew I was down to my last two pairs.

Throughout this period of not earning a dime, my landlady fed me every day. She made sure I had dinner to eat. When the Bible states in St. Matthew 6:25-33 . . . Take no thought for your life, what ye shall eat, or what ye shall drink . . . . But seek ye first the kingdom of God, and his righteousness; and all these things shall be added unto you. That is exactly what we should do, give God our all he deserves nothing less.

I had to finally accept that for myself, even though I never desired to be a divorcee and I wanted my marriage to work more than I desired my own life. I had to repent of this deadly obsession and give God my affections and my admiration. I gave up my marriage and eventually filed for a bill of divorcement after three years of marital separation. That closed the most deadly chapter of my life and released me into the realm of awesome possibilities. I serve an awesome, grandiose God and He was able to repair and restore this broken life. He did!!!!

Isaiah 54 became my favorite chapter in the Bible and this was my verse (Isaiah 54:5) For thy Maker is thine husband; the Lord of hosts is his name; and thy Redeemer the Holy One of Israel; The God of the whole earth shall he be called.

Since the Lord saved my life from the act of suicide, I have been exposed. I was a selfish woman with a hidden agenda in everything I did and I thought the Lord was my genie. He changed me from the inside out. He allowed me to see Him (Isaiah 6:1) high and lifted up! I came to realize that God is holy and worthy of praise and so I join with all the angels saying, Amen: Blessing, and glory, and wisdom, and thanksgiving, and honor, and power, and might, be unto our God forever and ever. Amen. Revelation 7:12

Since my journey began with the ministry in 2003, we were able to erect a school for high school for dropouts or delinquents. The ministry still stays true to its root of being a place where intercession is always heard. They also offer Christian counseling free of charge to whoever will come. I have since moved on to various projects and done many amazing things like preaching the word of God, participating in church outreach programs such as crusades and family life seminars in the capacity of 'Praying Evangelist'. I have seen people delivered and their circumstances and outlook on life changed because of prayer. I have seen demons driven back and lose their strongholds on many lives. I have seen people repent and become saved and baptized. I have seen God provide through miraculous ways. I have seen many battles fought and won by the Holy Spirit, and I have seen changes take place in the lives of my friends, family members and even strangers.

I have fasted for three days without food or drink and seen God heal cancer. I have prostrated my body and see God deliver, not just others but, also me. I am no longer the overzealous love seeker that I was. I have gone years without thinking about taking my life and feeling depressed for not doing it. I have endured not because I can, but because God has a plan for my life. This plan has taken me to relocate to the United States since August, 2009. Where it will take me after this, I do not know but, I can already guess it will be on a journey marked by God's amazing grace.

7 ADAM WHERE ART THOU?

"'For I know the plans I have for you,'
declares the Lord,
'plans to prosper you and not to harm you,
plans to give you hope and a future.
Then you will call upon me and come and
pray to me, and I will listen to you.
You will seek me and find me
when you seek me with all your heart.
I will be found by you,' declares the Lord,
'and will bring you back from captivity'."

Jeremiah 29: 11-14

This journey has not been an easy one. I have been changed from what I know to consider the things I do not know. Over time the Lord has spoken many times either directly or through messages from others. In September 2004, the Lord sent a message of restoration and renewal. He spoke emphatically that He was going to restore my mind and my body. I was going to be a virgin, and He, Himself would be my husband.

On Sunday, December 5, 2004, I received a very unusual call that made me cry. The speaker on the line spoke eloquently of a message she received in prayer from the Lord. For me, it was the promise of a second Adam, a virtuous man. The message consumed me and I was shaken to the core of my being that my Mighty God would be so kind that He would not withhold such a good gift from me.

So from that date onward, the Lord kept sending reminders of His promise of a second Adam and a restored life and possibly children, which to that date I had not conceived. The promise was comforting at first, but became eerie and I felt uncomfortable and stupid. How can I pray for a man I have never met; a man who would be my husband. It was a real stretch for me and did not seem logical and conclusive. This was an especially daunting task when I felt lonely, empty and needy, and I figured if a real man could not love me, then how a man conceived in my head would do any better.

So for months I fought with myself that I could not accept this promise as a prophetic word for my life and I stopped thinking about it for a while and stop hoping for it too. Then in June 2005, the message emerged; gentle reminders that there wasn't anything too hard for God to do and that His promises are true and He could be trusted. After all, He had proven Himself to be worthy. But, still I struggled mentally. I could not envision someone making me happy, being a good spouse and all the stories of marriages on the rocks were too familiar; therefore, I did not want to see the possibility of a happily ever after ending in store for me.

Thus, it continued to be a self induced difficult road to travel and I figured it best not to take the road less travelled. I had grown forlorn and cynical and days turned into weeks and weeks into months and then years passed.

In many ways I never believed I would find someone to love me. I thought the years of abuse had done its damage. I had been so angry at men all my life, my father for not being there for me and loving me and showing me how I should be treated as his daughter and as a woman. Angry at the men I have given my heart and my body to especially my ex-husband. But, I guess I was also angry at myself, why had I been this way. What was I searching for and where was I going to find it. It was even difficult to trust God, our Heavenly Father. He was supposed to be a God of love and infinite wisdom. But it was hard to trust Him, to love Him to want to be loved by Him.

God had promised me something I felt I didn't deserve or would ever have a chance to experience the passion and mystery of love, the love between a man and a woman.

Shortly, after my husband left me, I met a young man five years my junior. He spoke the way I expected my husband to speak to me; with tenderness, care and genuine warmth, but he was not to be my Adam. He was just something I needed at that time and it would not last. It couldn't! The friendship was what I needed, someone I could unburden my soul on and share how vulnerable and needy I was. How hurt I had been and how hurt I still was. How has a woman I forgot how to embrace my essence and hold on to my being, my sanity? This was at a time when I played Russian roulette with faith and suicide, with love and loss, with lust and dignity. I needed someone who could listen as I cried on the other end of the phone. I needed!

That chapter quickly closed and it was time to move on. Initially I thought he would repair the damage done to my heart but I soon realized he wasn't the one and I wasn't the one. Too often we think the other person is wrong for us but sometimes we are the wrong person too. That's a reality. I faced it and have been facing it, my truth.

I still was waiting for my ex-husband to come around and apologize and tell me he had made a terrible mistake and he was sorry he had left me and reclaim me and tell me how much he loved and needed me. I was still waiting. About three years after he left, it became apparent that I was waiting in vain. He had moved on physically and emotionally and I needed to do the same so I decided in my mind that it was time to file for divorce.

During that time when I had to come to terms with the imminent demise of my marriage and the reality that he would never come back I met a young man who was of like faith as I was who also was dealing with the reality of divorce being recently estranged from his wife of 5 plus years. We met at church and soon after talking we realized we had more than being Seventh-day Adventists in common, we were both spouses who had been betrayed and needed to settle the score with the finality of divorce. During the process of checking out our options legally we became fast and supportive friends.

Soon we were planning to get married as soon as we had finalized our divorces. However, it was not to be; while this man was one of the nicest men I had ever met it quickly fizzled and left us burnt. He had a heart of gold; my divorce was only made possible because he paid all my legal fees. He bought me clothes and helped me profoundly. He gave me financial assistance so that I could complete my Master's in Educational Psychology program. He made sure that my rent was paid and that food was on my table and really treated me like a princess. He was the only man to date that had shown me how I should be treated with love and care. However, I had not gotten over my pain and I lashed out unnecessarily and treated him like a scorned woman.

I hurt him with my words and belittled him with my bitterness. A man can do a lot of things to a woman that takes her years to get through or even get pass, but a woman can do the same and worst to a man. I did and I had to forgive myself because I had treated this man with impunity because of what someone else had done.

It's important to be honest at least with yourself. You can tell a lie but, it's very hard when you choose to live a lie. I acknowledged that I was wrong and quickly moved on. Shortly, after the break-up my divorce was finalized and I wept bitterly. I still had mixed feelings. I wanted this part of my life to be over but I wished it wasn't. Why did this have to happen and why do I still have emotions driven towards a man who didn't care if I existed or not? My ex-husband never gave me any indication that we could work towards reconciliation. Why was it so hard for me to accept that he never loved me or ever wanted me? It made me feel like less than a person, like there was something off with me.

I tried to shut down my emotions and decided that there were some things I couldn't control.

So I continued in ministry and struggled in life. In the summer of 2007 I worked with an organization as a counselor for troubled teens. I enjoyed it immensely, however, I was struggling. I still had not found anyone that I could pursue a meaningful relationship with so I stalled. As a sexual being I was dying, my body and my mind were out of sync the entire summer. Was it the summer heat or the fact that I had not had sex in four years? Whatever it was, I was sexually charged and in over drive. It was not long into the summer that I met a young man some 6 years my junior. He was in the Jamaican Army and had the body of a beast. We started having simple flirtatious conversations and at nights I would cry because I wanted this young man so badly, not relationally, but sexually. How could I, a woman of faith who had been involved in Christian ministry, feel the way I felt and make the decisions I did? It wasn't too long into our conversations that I noted that I was stifled. Something had to give and it did. Inevitably, I invited him to my room and into me. I slept with him repeatedly for a weekend and then walked away. I told him that I did not want a relationship with him but I wanted to feel like a woman again and I did.

To this point I have had many faith crises. This I thought, I could never recover from. I felt demoralized and evil. I had to face the fact that I was not only a spiritual being, I was also a sexual being and somehow the two had to coincide and be surrendered to the Living God in order for me to keep not just my faith, but my sanity. I went down in sack cloth and ashes not because I was so noble, but because the Holy Spirit convicted me and led me into the act of repentance, sincere sorrow for my sins. God pursued me once again and forgave me and cleansed me and I did not deserve it.

I was a woman who was seen as a 'prayer warrior' yet that's all I was—just a woman. I am nothing outside of God. He placed His own value on my life and made me into more than I was or thought I could ever be. It was a painful journey that I had to take those months following my fall from grace, but God gave the strength. I prayed honest prayers, not 'sugar coated' stuff. I genuinely told all to the Lord.

God worked on my self esteem, which all my life had been low. He gave me His esteem and told me to see myself through His eyes and not my own or even others. I lost my appetite for everything else for a while and once again I was consumed by God. My intercessions became more intense, because I had tasted that God is good. In time following that poor decision I have reclaimed my prayer and Bible study life and I have prayed continuous prayers for my Adam. Not the man I will choose, but the one God has chosen for me. Many suitors have since come and gone and now have been the 'one'. There was the doctor, no; the patient. Yet I believe in the plans of God and the ways of God which are passed finding out. God will do whatever He says He will do; simply because He, God cannot lie.

The promise kept emerging even though years have passed and I still believe. I am living and working in the United States of America, the land of great possibilities. This is a place where dreams and visions can come true. I am on the unconventional journey with God and I could not ask for anyone better, my Lord and I!

There have been so many twists and turns in my life. There was a time when I thought I had come to the end of my life and God asked me a simple question, "Will you give me your life?" I did, and although I have made many decisions which I have lived to regret, that is not one of them. As a matter of fact, that is the best decision I have ever made. So many things in life are fleeting, here today, gone tomorrow. There are so many fad and trends to follow, but the best and greatest trend is to follow Jesus. I do not know how He does it, but He can change your life even when you are at the lowest point of your life.

This experience with all its pain has been the single most precious of my life and if I should die today or tomorrow I take nothing away from God, He is truly amazing. He is an awe-inspiring God and the song writer did Him justice by simply saying 'He is God alone'.

And finally, I have met him. I have met my husband, the man I was born to love.

My Prayer

'Stop Resisting'

Father in the name of Jesus Christ of Nazareth I ask you to take control over all the areas of my life-body, mind, heart and soul—where I resist Your will and Your dominion (full control). I give You me; my imaginations, thoughts, desires, emotions, feelings (good/bad, positive/negative), ideas, beliefs, philosophies, dreams, aspirations, *wants, needs,* conclusions, *persuasions,* skepticism, bitterness, sarcasm, doubts, fears, unbelief, curses, blessings, joys, sorrows, pains, infirmities, inferiorities, superiorities, materialism, **family, friends**, lovers, crushes, lust, haters, regrets, mistakes, pride, malice, prejudice, swearing, blames, wishes, visions, jobs, poverty, wealth, successes, failures, apprehension and every other DIABOLICAL thing that makes me not want what You want in the name of Your precious Son Jesus Christ. Amen!

Tuesday, April 03, 2007

ABOUT THE AUTHOR

Allesley Officer is a Jamaican by birth and nationality. She is a Special Education teacher at a public charter school in Washington, DC. She is a member of and the former Public Relations Officer for a Non-Profit Outreach Ministry called Restoration NOW located in Saint Catherine, Jamaica.

She earned a Bachelor's degree in Special Education and completed her Master's degree in Educational Psychology both at the University of the West Indies, Mona Campus.

Her inspiration is the most prolific author of all times her personal companion, Jesus Christ. Her prayer is that God will become real and the desire for His second advent will take precedence in all our lives.

One of her aspirations is to go back to school and complete her doctorate in Child Guidance and Family Therapy. She ultimately wants to become a Family Counselor/Therapist. But then again, she could just keep writing books.

ABOUT THE BOOK

This is a straight forward journey into the life of a young girl growing up in Kingston, Jamaica.

She tells the tale of sexual abuse that led to compromise and exploits. She takes you into the raw emotions of her relationship with her father and her lovers and how she was eventually recaptured to live again.

There is hope, for her and for us all! Here in, lies the essence of her story, that the ray of hope is still available today for you and me. The human spirit is able to rise above life's challenges and heart breaks and soar like the Phoenix.